Department of Economic and Social Affairs
Division for Social Policy and Development
Family Unit

Family Indicators

United Nations
New York, 2003

NOTE

The designations employed and the presentation of the material in this publication do not imply the expression of any opinion whatsoever on the part of the Secretariat of the United Nations concerning the legal status of any country, territory, city or area or of its authorities, or concerning the delimitation of its frontiers.

ST/ESA/279

UNITED NATIONS PUBLICATION

Sales No. E.03.IV.4

ISBN 92-1-130225-0

PREFACE

As part of the approved work programme relating to families, and in view of the observance of the tenth anniversary of the International Year of the Family in 2004, the Division for Social Policy and Development of the Department of Economic and Social Affairs commissioned a study on family indicators to guide policy makers in their development of effective family policies. Marcel Fabri served as consultant.

CONTENTS

EXECUTIVE SUMMARY

Relying on a system of elaborate family indicators is necessary for the development of effective family policies. This paper attempts to look critically at current practice regarding indicators as well as the basic conditions necessary for the establishment of a comprehensive array of family indicators. In such a conceptual approach, a definition of the term "indicator" is central to the analysis, followed by a brief examination of the concept of family.

An indicator may be regarded as a quantitative tool for action whose usefulness is simply to indicate and therefore provide, in a quantitative form, an approximate view of reality. To achieve that, it is necessary to define the concepts of the family and its proxy, the household.

Two approaches, one statistical and the other sociological, are available to assist in finding a definition of the family. They are, however, opposing ones. While one approach seeks to unify, the other is designed to expose the differences. Finding a single definition is hindered by the diversity of families in both developed and developing countries.

It thus seems justified to wonder what the usual approach to family indicators should be. The relevance of censuses as an easy source for data is appraised, as well as the possible secondary use of surveys, although they have not been developed for studying the family. Caution is recommended: the set of available indicators is not homogeneous, and should be divided into three groups:

1. Static indicators descriptive of the household;

2. Dynamic indicators that take into account changing relationships;

3. Functional indicators for policy approaches.

In order to define the family, the global perception of the concept of family must be broken down. The necessary classification could be a model or typology. Various proposals and their shortcomings are examined. The main characteristics that eventually emerge are what an indicator should represent. Three major features respond to a global picture of the household, leading to the conceptualization of the family:

1. The **structure** or the shape that households are exhibiting worldwide. Structures are numerous and not limited to the nuclear family model.

1

They can only be grasped through a typology that would refer to the dyad as the smallest significant unit in the household;

2. **Residence** is a basic element in the definition of the household, with its patterns and rules that differ from one cultural context to another, requiring a few illustrations and resulting in a reduced listing of types;

3. The **size** of a household is a numerical source of information that is linked to a major indicator.

Associated indicators that show a high correlation with size variations are added to illuminate the concept of family and explain the changes that have occurred in the family. These associated indicators relate to fertility, mortality, marriage, age distributions (first marriage, age at first birth), disruption and dissolution of the family, and migration.

The study shows that the real meaningful unit for the creation of family indicators is the household, while the family remains a fluctuating concept, its form and content reflecting a social and political choice.

INTRODUCTION

> To be completely realistic and take account of everything at once is hardly the object. Suppose it were possible to make a simulation that corresponded exactly with what occurs, with all the variables of the real world operating; one would not have a simulation at all, we would be simply reproducing the entity simulated. If one could go that far in the direction of realism, one would have a multiplicity of empirical data, but then one would have to start from the beginning to make simpler models in order to draw understandable conclusions.
>
> Nathan Keyfitz[1]

What is a family today? It is commonly assumed that in every society there is a group of persons called "family". However, apart from the fact that the family has been viewed for decades, if not for centuries, as one of the core institutions of society, which it helps to shape, what society currently exhibits does not correspond to the concept of family as it is commonly assumed to exist. Nevertheless, despite its diversity, the family remains a basic social unit that provides a rational environment for any attempt to improve the welfare of a population. Thus, it is essential to know what a family is: it is necessary to find a proper definition that takes into account not only its perennial attributes but also the continuous alterations that the institution has undergone. Determining the conditions by which the family has changed as an evolving model would provide an adequate framework to enhance the development of society.

Decision makers and policy makers need to operate within a well-defined territory in order to identify the beneficiaries of the improvements they seek to introduce. Since time is always of the essence, tools are needed that will quickly provide them with an integrated view of the situation and of the object they plan to modify. Indicators are designed to fulfil this purpose. To start with, it is necessary to know what to expect from an indicator and what elements have been used up to now as family indicators.

---

[1] In *Family Demography: Methods and Their Applications*, John Bongaarts, Thomas Burch and Kenneth Wachter, eds. (Oxford, United Kingdom, Clarendon Press, 1987).

I. THE QUANTITATIVE APPROACH TO FAMILY

A. THE CONCEPT OF THE INDICATOR

An indicator approach is basically a quantitative approach. It may be defined by employing a statistical technique that proceeds on the basis of predefined categories. These categories, which are assumed to be universal, allow a comparison of homogeneous data from different groups. An indicator will be meaningful and therefore justified if the initial concept to which it applies is well defined and unambiguous. This requires specifying not only what it is, including its limitations, but also to what it applies. It is within this context that indicators may be designed. What, therefore, are indicators and why use them?

No formal definition of "indicator" is available; however, it is commonly interpreted as a quantitative substitute that is used to represent an elementary characteristic of a phenomenon. In addition, it also summarizes a single or a mixed aspect of a social reality, whether this is the unit under study or an associated element that identifies it. Although the indicator appears as a figure, it does not claim to provide a measure of its object; this is not its function.

The indicator, as suggested by its name, is simply used to indicate (Galtung and others, 1978). Devising an indicator for a phenomenon does not mean an attempt to measure, but to find a quantitative representation that characterizes the object (including its possible shapes or transformations) or event. It is in this sense that it could be said that measurement is not its function. In the same way that measurement focuses on precise knowledge, the indicator is supposed to be a tool for action—addressing the necessity to provide quick information on the approximate state of the elements that constitute the phenomenon and/or point out relations that should be changed. It could, therefore, be viewed as an image or a reflection; as an icon suggesting an analogy; or even as a clue to an underlying variable regularly linked with the object but not directly measurable. In this sense, it could also be regarded as a proxy. Although the indicator does not measure, since measurement is not its objective, as quantitative information it is generally based on initial measures and, for its relevance, on the quality of measurement. Therefore, even if accuracy is not a definite requirement for an indicator, its bases must be accurate because any attempt to measure depends on a theory of the object to be appraised.

5

This leads to the question of the family. "Family" as a category has to be defined. The qualitative approach of sociology is in this case the necessary complement to censuses, ethnological surveys and empirical interpretation.

The concept of family lends itself simultaneously to more than one meaning. It is also multidimensional. While in developed countries the family has long been regarded by demographers, among others, as a single and stable model based on the evidence of a legally married couple and its eventual offspring, it has recently been diversifying beyond all expectations. The developing countries, on the other hand, have always exhibited a wide variety of family structures. These structures refer to the display of elements and to the multidimensional aspect of the concept. Keeping this essential characteristic in mind, it should be emphasized that, while multiple meanings and dimensions are at the core of the quantitative approach to family, the complexity of the universe of the family is not limited to a single sphere, but exists in multiple contexts.

Given the diversity of cultural and social environments, different organizational patterns interact together under specific demographic and sociological conditions. This means that any attempt to formulate general views should be designed along the lines of the observed diversity of the social and demographic conditions that have shaped the content and form of the family.

Usually, sets of data are provided that express in figures the evolution or the comparability of detailed characteristics of a phenomenon, in an attempt to capture a particular pattern or behaviour of the object of study, quantify it and in some way give it an objective existence or autonomy.

This must be considered as the initial step in forecasting its future trends, since action is expected to bring a change—a desired change when it results from a policy. Most of the time these measures, taken as carefully as possible, are summarized into an index, which bears the notion of "indicating", but whose objective is more to provide a synthetic measure, though imperfect, for purposes of analysis. Having this in common with the measure on which it is based, the indicator is expected from a technical point of view to reproduce, on repeated occasions, the same results: a condition of reliability. This should not prevent it from varying significantly with the real object, as a reliable quantity is also responsive to change.

What eventually should determine the requirements for the indicator is its relevance to its projected use: its validity. This refers to two related conditions: one concerns the appropriate representation of the concept by the indicator, and the other its fitness for performing the specific function that has been assigned to it. Its final use is always in conjunction with an identified system at large and the change this undergoes or is subjected to.

An indicator is a tool for policies—in this case, for social policies—and should therefore be strictly operational.

B. The concept of family

Concepts are vital in any analysis. That refers not only to basic concepts, but also to related ones and to the selection and definition of relevant factors and events. Whenever one seeks to depict a phenomenon quantitatively, one has at least to determine what is to be depicted and to what extent the representation fits the reality unambiguously.

During the past decades, there has been a renewal of interest in the family from many disciplines. It has become an object of focus for an interdisciplinary approach, after having been studied separately by demographers, sociologists, jurists, anthropologists and economists as well as by specialists in education and health (one aspect of multidimensionality).

Society is not built upon individuals or on groups, but on interactions between groups. This means that interrelationships are of the essence. This would also justify why, in attempting to study the family, many disciplines are involved (Fabri, 1982).

The fundamental transformation in family structure that has occurred more recently in most developed countries and is now threatening traditional family models in less developed countries, under the label of modernization, has become a challenge to any easy and single definition of this social institution. Defining the subsystem and understanding how and why it evolved so fast and so deeply are actually the main focus of the recent development of family studies in sociology. Although any deliberate attempt to change an institution and its framework calls for knowledge, policy makers cannot wait for an ever-evolving model to be devised. They need pertinent and immediate guidance to take action and agree on a definition and concept deemed to be optimal for the welfare of society.

Two ways of defining the family can be distinguished. Again, the two approaches are not independent, but merely differ in focus, each one expressing a complementary point of view. On the one hand, the family appears as a basic institution and the major constituent of society. On the other hand, a family, in its nuclear form, is traditionally a group of people linked by marriage, legally or customarily regulated, and their dependants, based on either consanguinity or adoption. Although both approaches are equally important, each one calls for a different perspective and therefore specific methods of analysis. One refers to family as a unit in social interaction, and the other focuses on intrinsic family relations, or the interactions among the individuals constituting the unit. The question arises, however, of what the family looks like today. Families at present exist in different forms, most of them distinct from the traditional pattern of the nuclear family.

As an institution, the family has been commonly regarded as an entity that is greater than the sum of its parts. It has been identified as a focal point for social decisions, either resulting from a consensus among its members or based on decision-making by the head of the family. The latter formula, however, is less and less a reality as the growing independence of family members makes it more and more difficult.

In addition, cohabitation has proved increasingly to be a temporary or permanent substitute for marriage. Never-married mothers and single fathers as well as homosexual parenting have become more common, hampering the task of finding a universal definition of the family. Even when the social relations of the family are considered, an appropriate definition is essential to depict the prevailing situation and the way it is likely to evolve.

The **family** is defined primarily with reference to relationships that pertain to or arise from marriage, reproduction or adoption, all of which are regulated by law or custom. It seems at first glance that no objective criteria can be found to define a family. Shared residence and income, in the absence of legal and/or biological evidence, do not suffice to determine the reality of a family without considering affective links, and these are as diverse as individuals. For practical purposes, it is important to come up with a definition based on as few common features as possible, searching for common denominators without reducing the cultural diversity of family types. The demographic definition of the family may be the most general and objective, but at the price of simplification, so that specific characteristics are lost.

As a unit in demographic studies representing all or part of a household, a **statistical family** or **census family** generally consists of all members of a household who are related through blood, adoption or marriage. A statistical family cannot comprise more than one household, although a household may include more than one family. Hence, the factors that contribute to the formation and dissolution of the family are mostly dynamic events. Studying the transformation of the family requires, nevertheless, familial groups that are initially stable, and has led to advocacy of a restrictive definition considering only legitimate families (Ryder, 1977). Since then, however, the extent of the alteration of family structures has justified the adoption of a different position, taking into account de facto families and unions in addition to married couples.

To facilitate data availability, the quantitative approach to family employs an approximation, considered as its statistical nearest substitute: the household, which emphasizes residence and income. The definition of a household is based on residence and the shared cost of living together in the same place, implying the notion of income without specifying affective relationships among members of the group.

A **household** is a socio-economic unit that consists of individuals who live together (referring restrictively to private households, consisting of one or several persons who are members of the household, as opposed to collective households such as barracks or convents). According to the definition, which has been recommended as an international standard, a household consists of a group of individuals who share living quarters (a statistical abstraction denoting housing accommodations appropriate for occupation by one household) and their principal meals (IUSSP, 1982). Among the members of the household, one of them will be the head of the household or householder (it may be, but does not necessarily have to be, the main wage earner). The term "headship" is frequently encountered, as in **headship ratio**, the ratio of the number of heads of households by age, sex and other characteristics to the corresponding categories in the population (IUSSP, 1982).

While most dwellings contain only one household, the relative independence of the members who are working corresponds to a relative independence of income and a partial contribution to common household expenses. In this case, a common dwelling seems to be the main criterion for defining family life. However, increasing labour mobility may divide the couple or group of persons depending on a common income between two or more residences, seen as secondary and transitory residences. Given current residence and parental patterns and rules, there is always a possibility of an arrangement between norms and practice. The following patterns and rules were fundamental to the formation of the group, to the extent that they used to determine inclusion in the group: location of residence; procedure for inheritance; conditions to gain access to the means of production; and ways to meet a conjugal partner. While these patterns and rules for households were once rather rigid, there are now many possible variations.

Until recently, in industrial countries the family was considered not to differ very much from the household. With increasing change in the structure of families and the occurrence of new factors, it is becoming less and less true. Nevertheless, there is a high correlation between families and households in regard to their size.

A single-parent family, whether headed by the father or by the mother, is not an exception any more. A single person (unmarried, widowed or divorced) should constitute a household without forming a family, although the household definition eliminates him/her.

It should be further noted that the statistical concept of the household is not otherwise affected if the residing unit is a same-sex couple, whereas on the policy level this concept of family requires an official acknowledgement resulting from a political decision.

Despite the appearance of permanence and constant references to the nuclear unit, family has never been a permanent institution. Various types of families have always coexisted, even throughout Western history.[2] More recently, the shape of the family has evolved more rapidly, leading to deeper changes in its inner and external relationships and causing concern as to what a family should be, what its purpose ought to be and how transitory its current stage is. The formal acknowledgement of its shape and its legal status remain dependent upon social change. That, however, does not mean that the current definition of the family is accepted by public opinion. Thus, describing what a family is involves defining and explaining both past and present, in order to identify the mechanisms involved in its formation and transformation. Only when some clarity has been established regarding its complex course of change will it be possible to create the instruments that are capable of amending the notion of family. Family indicators can only be conceptualized as soon as this clarification has been achieved. It is not possible to demonstrate that social change is either good or bad since such a stance depends on the respective political points of view. Therefore, no objective criteria are available to judge the occurrence of the extended family, the nuclear family or simple cohabitation, since these different family forms are born out of social structures that evolve in response to new factors and new sets of relationships, which in turn shape to some extent new conventions and norms. Political change involving a loosening of the social structure may, however, affect the shape and size of families, as can be clearly observed in Eastern Europe, where fragmentation of the traditional nuclear family is on the rise, resulting in increasing numbers of orphans or abandoned children.

From one part of the world to another, cultural variations may lead to the selection of different indicators. Infant and child mortality is an issue of much importance in developing countries, in contrast to recent experiences in the developed countries. In addition, third world countries remain con-

---

[2]In England, at the peak of the Victorian era, the writer Wilkie Collins openly supported (as an exceptional non-conformist) two unsanctified families. It is, however, paradoxical that this domestic openness did not find its way into his work, which was more orthodox than that of his friend Trollope, whose work was much more in accordance with his life in his society, and far more so than that reflected in Ibsen's *A Doll's House* and J. S. Mill's *The Subjection of Women*, which were both published at about the same time.

cerned with the number of children who continue to live with their parents once grown up, while this information seems to be of lesser interest to developed countries. For instance, among the Mossi of Burkina Faso, family is patrilocal but matrilineal: the son lives with his father but inherits from his maternal uncle, thereafter leaving the paternal clan (Gruenais, 1981). In other parts of Africa, the wife traditionally lives with her family with her children, while the husband, who lives in a separate residence, has to visit her. Thus, multiple variations make it impossible to define the "traditional family" in different parts of the developing world. Rapid urbanization and growing globalization are causing current family models to shift towards the nuclear family, allowing statisticians to collect data about households. The process is, however, slow.

Shared meals and income are part of the household definition and help define the concept. Much as gross national product (GNP) may be qualified not only by its size but also by its level of distribution among the population, data on the distribution of household income are essential for comparison and aggregation. How the income is generated is as important as the comparison of economic and cultural differences in regard to income.

In the developed countries (including the parts of developing countries that are viewed as integrated into the global economy, either because they are urban or because of their interdependence with the global economy[3]) both income and expenditure are increasingly diversified. Such changes as technical progress in the modes of payment and banking practices that give wives and even teenagers access to bank accounts, as compared with a single common budget with only one person responsible for its use, have assisted in this process. This diversification is both a factor in and a consequence of the growing individual autonomy pervading all forms of the family and fragmenting household income.

---

[3]China, Hong Kong S.A.R. and Singapore are classic examples of such assimilation to the urban global culture, while in most Latin American countries some segments of society are part of the subsistence economy and others operate in the most advanced sectors of the economy. The presence of oil in Nigeria has also resulted in the existence of a mixed society.

II. THE USUAL APPROACH TO FAMILY INDICATORS

Given that an acceptable definition for family indicators can be identified and agreed upon, the next question is, "What should an indicator indicate about family?" It has been stated that indicators are statistics-based and dependent upon the existence of reliable data. However, the organization of statistical data-gathering presents serious challenges, since neither the industrialized countries nor those of the third world have adjusted their techniques for the collection of information since the departure from the nuclear family.

All family indicators cannot be considered the same. It is possible to distinguish among functional types, which may be identified as follows:

(1) **Descriptive**. These indicators are based on a static approach, taking into account the most noticeable characteristics of the household to recreate its perceptible reality, including its structure and size.

(2) **Dynamic**. This approach takes into account the changes that models have undergone as well as the determinants and consequences of change. That implies an explanatory approach, which considers the family as a social and economic unit of a given society (indicators focus on fertility, mortality and migration, together with income, employment and occupation).

(3) **Policy approach**. This suggests a need for operational indicators, not necessarily different from the other two categories, but targeted to capture deliberate changes that may have an impact on particular or related aspects of the family. More often than not, the indicators will be only indirectly related to the family. This is the case with housing conditions, the type of expenditure within the household or the current prices of food products or other commodities (Fabri, 1990).

A. CURRENT SOURCES OF INDICATORS AND TYPOLOGY OF HOUSEHOLD/FAMILY

1. Censuses and surveys

The practical advantage of an indicator is that it can be an easy substitute for an in-depth analysis and measurement of the family. Data should

12

therefore be readily available, and the census seems to be the primary source for developing such an approximation. Whatever the method of organizing the computation, the key to a successful outcome will be the extent to which simplification, which does not include biases, can be found. As a primary source of data collection, the census provides secondary or related concepts that eventually help to characterize the family.

An indicator is useful if it permits comparison of the situation at two instances and provides an understanding of the process of modification by showing the factors explaining the variations between the two situations. An immediate methodological consequence is that the description of the initial stock and flow of variations must correspond.

Consequently, two approaches appear workable: one approach uses flows that are exogenous to censuses (vital statistics that show the change of events) in order to modify the initial stock. Usage could also be made of transitional probabilities (death, marriage, divorce, fertility etc.), adopting the concept of the family as basic unit and also implying that a single typology of families would be agreed upon as a standard classification.

A second approach, the comparison of two censuses, avoids using exogenous flows. The household becomes the basic unit, and the flows would be observed by breaking down the main types into sub-types. For example, groups of one-person households would be analysed by using the variation in the distribution of these households from one census to another, according to marital status and age group. One could show, for example, that in the age group 30 to 49 years, the group of households composed of one man alone is largely the consequence of divorce. However, a typology of households would be necessary, taking into account the composition of the family and not only the presence or absence of isolated persons.

A census is in general based on geography, and its primary unit is a residence, the dwelling. Preferably, the informant is the head of the household, defined by the United Nations as that person who is acknowledged as such by the other members (United Nations, 1980). Once a reality, the notion of household headship has become vague and fluctuating, and it is practically meaningless in the developed countries.

Sample surveys provide other sources of data, even as a secondary analysis. The Demographic and Health Survey (DHS) has at times been tentatively used for devising indicators, with a focus on the developing countries (Bongaarts, 2001), where data, in particular about the family, are scarce and not too reliable. While this approach is promising, the sample drawn for the interviews is based neither on households nor on the number of adults within a household, but on women of reproductive age. Consequently, although the information collected about members of the household may be detailed enough to provide data on such items as age, sex and residential status, the results may not be representative of the household structure and therefore do not allow any generalization.

2. *Typology of family or household*

Precise definitions of main as well as related concepts are prerequisites to quantification. Whether in regard to its substance or its inner behavioural processes, the family or its statistical analogue, the household, exhibits shapes that are as distinct as they are multiple. The concept must be broken down into categories that are mutually exclusive and in such numbers that as many attributes as possible are taken into account. It is necessary to build up a typology, which is an ideal classification or model. Forms that map the possible levels of complexity have to be designed like a grid that operates through regrouping to fit each specific case. Each time, content should be reappraised in the light of specific contexts, as the concept may conceal a number of distinct meanings. Generalization would create a model for action, but would in no way represent a valid classification conforming to reality. Construction of a typology of the family or household should be seen as an exercise that justifies necessary action; it is a tool rather than a real mapping of the family concept. A parallel can be found in the econometric model, which is actually a referent or substitute for reality.

From a practical point of view, leaving aside the construction of taxonomies and the search for numerical classification, the classification criteria in the typology of households within which families are being defined have to correspond to the data collected by the census. These data are already classified as a result of the census analysis, but only those deemed relevant to the household would be likely to be taken into account as a conceptual category and as a component of the typology. These elements, ranging from data on fertility, income and occupation to data on housing conditions, should be closely associated with the family and should provide a basis for its socio-economic assessment. The high degree of correlation that the variables maintain with the household or family are to be seen as explanatory of the changes they undergo, while distribution according to age, gender, space units and time are specifying conditions and attributes of the household members.

The United Nations currently employs a household classification based on family structure (see annex III). Four basic household types are identified:

(*a*) One-person household;

(*b*) Nuclear household;

14

(*c*)   Extended household;

(*d*)   Composite household.

In this case, the term "family" means the nuclear family, which includes couples with or without children, as well as single parents with children.

Many authors think that one of the first tasks for the study of the family is to provide for a sound typology (Roussel, 1980). In France, for the censuses of 1968 and 1975 three demographic units were used: individual, family and household, but with reference to the "head of household". This prevented sorting out households according to specific characteristics without proceeding through several cross-tabulations. The example given by Roussel refers to the household composed of one married couple and their children, which could only be enumerated by cross-tabulating the following information on the **household with only one family**:

(*a*)   Without any other isolated people;

(*b*)   With the presence of the spouse of the head of the household;

(*c*)   The couple must be legally married;

(*d*)   With at least one child.

This information, however, proceeds from the head of the household, whose definition, as mentioned above, is that person who is acknowledged as such by the other members (United Nations, 1980). Again, this is a notion that little by little has become meaningless in developed countries.

On the basis of the following four criteria, Roussel (1980) proposed the following typologies for families and households (see annexes I and II):

(*a*)   Number of families in the household (0, 1, 2, 3 and more);

(*b*)   The presence or absence of isolated people:

Case 1: no isolated person

Case 2: one isolated person who is an ascendant or a descendant aged 25 years or over

Case 3: other constellations of isolated people;

(*c*)   Family structure:

Case 1: one couple

Case 2: one couple with at least one child under 25 years old

Case 3: one parent (i.e., without spouse) with at least one child under 25 years old;

(*d*) Legitimacy of the couple.

The classification criteria in the typology of households, within which families are being defined, have to correspond to the data collected by the census. This also implies that prior to any analysis, a definition of family has been selected, which is a practical definition in accordance with statistical requirements. At any given moment, not only are there many types of family groups, but also rapid changes from one to another. Possible criteria include the following:

(*a*) Heterogeneity—The easiest kind of analysis assumes that all members of a group can be seen to have identical transition probabilities, as in the life table. There is an initial individual inequality in mortality. Heterogeneity is even greater in divorce. There is a higher probability for most age groups for family dissolution than for death. It is a given that everyone will die one day, but some individuals marry and divorce many times, whereas others never divorce.

(*b*) Lack of independence—A correlation exists often among demographic inputs, such as differentials in mortality (poor families of poor health with more offspring).

(*c*) Non-marriage—There is a continuum that ranges from life-long registered marriage to temporary arrangements for economizing on rent, raising the question as to which of these should be counted as stable unions.

B. HOUSEHOLD AND FAMILY INDICATORS

1. *Household structures*

Just as a worker may appear in many different guises—wage labourer or consumer, middle class or unemployed—the term "peasant" is all-encompassing and hides many deep distinctions. The groups may fall into categories as different as the so-called "primitive" or "archaic" communities and the peasants, who are identified by their social status and their function. It has become customary to distinguish peasants from primitives by opposing rural populations, which are subject to the dictates of a superordinate State, from rural-dwellers who live outside the confines of such a political structure. The first are peasants, the second are not (Wolf, 1969).

Although solidarity is an essential characteristic in defining a community, people can be to some extent deprived of it. However, this does not spring from their natural environment or from a territory, whether or not controlled by a political structure (Tilly, 1964). In particular, the cohesion of the household owes much to its location within its own territory, its residence, which may also be affected by the type of environment. This is exemplified by the moving residence of the nomads, which includes the space, the soil fertility and the isolation of the habitat. Therefore, geographical and social environments are a factor in the household propensity to transform.

The material, cultural and institutional aspects of social structures are a powerful determinant of substructures and group behaviours. In the nineteenth century, workers and peasants were groups of people defined by the external conditions that were transforming society: the industrial revolution; the increasing dependency of the countryside on urban growth; and the resulting disruption of the household and family.

The importance of social stratification alludes to multiple stratifications, based on economic hierarchy, such as "class"; on prestige or "status"; or on political power (the party), according to the basic distinction proposed by Max Weber (see Loriaux, 1982). Those stratifications extended to the whole of society. As traditional structures (the values that sustained strict partition within society) progressively weakened, a wider population penetrated deeper into the ranks of power, resulting in the rise of economic groups to which the State was increasingly subordinated.

The changes that occurred in the shape of households, and the loosening of links and legal bonds regarding family patterns, corresponded to the increasing democratization of societies, resulting in higher social tolerance.

William Goode predicted that whenever the economic system expanded through industrialization, family patterns would change, extended kinship ties would weaken, lineage patterns would dissolve and a trend towards some form of the conjugal system would generally begin to appear—that is, the nuclear family would become a more independent kinship unit (Bongaarts, 2001). This has certainly been true for developed countries, but the situation is less clear in developing countries. Increasing internal migration has brought young men into the urban centres, depleting rural areas. A few of them have returned to the countryside to marry, but many others have remained in the city, reuniting with their wives and children. In the latter case, they have apparently founded nuclear families. Given the flow of migrants and the strength of the traditional kinship ties, extended households have begun to bypass in size their traditional size in the village. This situation may well be transitory, but the transition takes a long time to complete and must be taken into account as a current reality.

These considerations justify separate treatment for the developing regions and the industrialized countries. Although the nuclear family is considered as a social unit to be found everywhere, in all societies at all times, this is actually not so: using a classic survey conducted by Nimkoff and Middleton containing over 549 different cultures and representing coverage of nearly all given cultural variations, A. Michel showed a prevalence of the nuclear family in 45 per cent of societies, but a prevalence of 55 per cent for the extended family (see Gruenais, 1981). With the increasing variety of families in the developed countries, it appears that these proportions would be even more dramatic today. Even though a comparison of the survey findings based on genuine cultural attributes with more recent data covering some countries would be difficult, if not impossible, the trend towards the decline of the nuclear family type is amply confirmed. While these indications come from separate data sources, all point in the same direction: in most regions the percentage of ever-married women aged 15-19 has decreased, and the postponement of marriage has increased, especially in developed countries (approximately between the periods 1975-1984 and 1985-1997). In addition, the number of marriages has fallen; cohabitation and informal unions have become more common, even in developing countries; and the proportions of divorced and separated people have increased practically everywhere. Consequently, the percentage of births to unmarried women has surged in the developed countries and has also substantially increased elsewhere, during roughly the same time period (United Nations, 1995 and 2000).

According to Wolf (1966), the nuclear family is further conceptually subdivided. Several sets of dyadic relationships can be identified as common to areas in both developed and developing countries:

(*a*) **Sexual dyads**, underlining the relation between a man and a woman and which, once socially acknowledged, lead to (*b*);

(*b*) **Conjugal dyads**, emphasizing the legal couple;

(*c*) The relation between mother and child determining the **maternal dyad**;

(*d*) The relation between siblings (brother and sister) resulting in another set of dyads;

(*e*) The **paternal dyad** characterizing the relationship between father and child.

With the exception of the paternal dyads, all these elementary units are factual and well established. In the case of the father-child relation, paternity cannot be directly perceived or confirmed. Confirmation is at the second degree, either legally or within a legal situation, such as for the father to belong to the conjugal dyad to which the child's mother belongs. This explains why in many societies the influence of the mother's brother, the child's uncle, supersedes the father's rights and influence.

By basing the typology on dyads instead of on the nuclear family, while eventually including the nuclear family's occurrence, it becomes possible to allow traditional models from non-Western cultures to be taken into account. Nuclear families can be built on dyads, representing the simplest case of an extended family and emphasizing the natural link that exists between the mother and her children. One has to bear in mind that the purpose of a typology is to allow for comparisons between various systems.

It should also be remembered that in past Western civilizations the creative event founding a family was—in appearance—the marriage as a union between two individuals. What it used to consecrate was the union of two families in the widest sense of kinship. This situation still exists in Africa and in traditional cultures elsewhere, where the marriage proceeds to a transfer of wealth, in this case from the bridegroom's family to the bride's family through the dowry, which confers the right of paternity to the newly wed.

The paradox is that, although the dyads may be the most basic components of a household everywhere, they are actually not to be found as such. Although they symbolize the establishment of households, they practically never exist in isolation, except recently in the developed countries. Except for one-person households, families and households consist of dyads that differ only marginally in both developed and developing countries, despite distinct contexts and circumstances.

Bearing in mind the reliance on a system of key indicators to assess a country's situation with respect to family structures, a description of the family is necessarily based on statistics describing the household because these are the only sets of data currently available. As a prerequisite, a typology of the household must be based on simple indicator proposals. A standard classification that would cover, though in a limited way, the wide diversity of legal and customary models that societies exhibit all over the world could be achieved by using subcategories that depart from the new tradition created in developed countries during the twentieth century.

Household structure is of fundamental importance, since it not only defines its current situation but also heralds present and future changes. Numbers and proportions for each group in a selected category should result in a portrayal of the household. A non-exclusive proposal for classification of households by type could be as follows:

(*a*) Single-family unit:

- One person: transitory subcategory composed of:

    Never married;

    Divorced/separated;

Widowed;

- One-parent families with dependent children (dependent children under 15 or 15 to 18/24 in full-time education);

- Married couples with no children;

- Unmarried adult couples in cohabitation with no children;

- Married couples with dependent children;

(*b*) More complex households:

- Groups of non-married adults other than couples (siblings, brother and sister or other kin);

- One family with dependent and independent children but no others in household;

- Other complex households.

Each group can be further specified by sex and by age.

The above classification does not focus on "residence" in order to identify family units. For instance, unmarried couples with children are counted as a one-parent family, failing to specify the heterogeneity of the couple's bonds, while childless couples might also include parents whose offspring have become independent, whether or not the children continue to live in the same household. However, these variations are taken into account in the complex household.

2. *Patterns and rules of residence*

The definition of "household" rests primarily on the residence. Shared dwellings are the basis of a census. Rules of residence have, therefore, a definite impact on the household structure. However, a great deal of differentiation is concealed under the heading of "residence": no distinction is made between centralized and non-centralized or patrilineal and matrilineal societies. In addition, recent aspects of modernization have had even greater effects on families than the economic changes that influenced households everywhere (Goody, 1990). While in developed countries censuses pay attention to geographical and conceptual residences—enumerating buildings, dwellings and occupation—in other regions of the globe, residence and culture are tightly intermingled, in particular in Africa where, compared with Eurasia, population is relatively sparse and kin ties are widely dispersed (Goody, 1990). However, huge agglomerations like Ibadan in Nigeria, populated now by millions of inhabitants, have been growing rapidly. With unplanned urban and suburban districts resulting in excessive residential

20

slums that represent up to 75 per cent of the city, Ibadan remains impervious to any census based on residence.

Residence rules might not distinguish the family from the household, because members of the family do not necessarily live in the same household. Rules are set by a pattern of traditional reliance on lineage and help establish the processes of transferring inheritance, remarrying and determining the status of kin.

The following example concerning the Nakanai communities of New Britain Island in Papua New Guinea (Goodenough, 1968) illustrates the difficulty of agreeing on what is or what is not a case of matrilocal residence. A remarried man lives with his three sons from the previous marriage, in a hamlet whose only clear pattern of residence is that a man regularly brings his wife to live in the hamlet where his father is residing. His eldest son is married and lives in the same household. Residence is patrilocal. However, the man's late first wife belonged to a matrilineal lineage, which owns the house and land on which the extended family lives. In addition, the first wife's sister lives nearby with her husband and children, like other women of this lineage residing in the hamlet with their husbands and children. Thus, the father actually moved into a matrilocal residence with his first wife and was able to remain in the house with his son after her death because he had no sister living there. If his sister had shared the residence where he lived with his first wife, he would have had to build a house (neo-local residence) because of the prohibition on adult brothers and sisters sleeping under the same roof. Thus, instead of a patrilocal residence as first assumed, the example becomes one of an avunculocal extended family, more specifically through the son, who now lives where his maternal uncles would be if he had any. None of this information is provided by the census. Any interpretation from census data overlooking such elements, which are not directly available, would be erroneous. It would preclude any attempt to identify patterns of residence in a society and would prevent classifying the residence of individual couples. Additional genealogical and sociological information would be needed.

The extent to which these traditional types of residence affect the construction of indicators is still to be determined. The possibility of working with indicators designed on a conventional basis, even when erroneous, is not so unusual when the objectives are being considered. If the indicator were a measure, the exemplified misinterpretation would be very serious. However, since it has already been qualified as a quantitative tool for launching action, practical consequences might not occur and interpretation might not actually be a problem. On this basis, there seem to be conflicting objectives between indicator and knowledge-oriented approaches. On the one hand, in order to make the comparison, what counts is the commonalities in situations and conditions. On the other hand, it is important to extract the most genuine and accurate characteristics that illustrate the real identity of the object presented for analysis.

In terms of a cost-benefit analysis, the search for a rigorously exact interpretation when creating indicators seems inadequate in comparison to the effort it would require. However, the function of the potential indicator has to be specified and emphasized, as, for instance, in the formulation of a housing policy that would disregard these rules and patterns of residence. This could result in a complete failure of welfare relocation projects, as the new building blocks would definitely remain vacant. Similar effects were noted in Iraq, where newly built agglomerations designed for a better de-limitation of property were not used because they did not take into account the disruption of usual social connections.

In this respect, it may also be useful to remember that most pro-grammes for family planning, despite relentless efforts to reach rapid results, had to wait practically two decades to reach effective changes in fertility. Reasons for this delay can be found in the failure to consider the context of application, which was mostly the family in its diversity. Technically these programmes had been impressive but, when applied from a Western point of view to societies that could neither understand them nor abide by them, put their communities and values in jeopardy. Shifting to a social and indi-vidual health orientation helped to close the gap and achieved results, since it recognized that it was paramount to take the specificity of each social environment as well as the male partner into account. Bearing this example in mind, and considering that indicators should be a basis on which policies would be designed, disregarding distinct realities would have serious con-sequences in formulating policies that focus on families. It might therefore be useful to try to disentangle the rules of residence by viewing them from the perspective of co-residence. The alternate residence classification that Bohannan (1968) proposed regarding basic relationships might fulfil this purpose. Five primary relationships predominantly support the household:

(*a*) **Husband-wife**. This is the typical pattern for the developed countries, which encourages the man to build a new house for his nuclear family, his wife and children, under a "neolocal" pattern. A few cases may appear ambiguous, such as in the north-eastern part of Nigeria, where the Hausa are basically patrilocal. A husband there can, however, recognize the reluctance of his spouse to become—as often expected—a servant to her mother-in-law. The husband would then settle in the neighbourhood and found a new domestic unit while keeping his ties with his father's house.

(*b*) **Father-son**. In central Nigeria, a departure from the Hausa is il-lustrated by the Tiv, who are strictly patrilocal and would never leave their father's compound, because "they can get a new wife any time, but have only one set of parents".

(*c*) **Mother-daughter**. Among the Hopi of Arizona, it may happen that a man builds a house, but does not own it. Devolution rules follow a mother-to-daughter scheme. The man is a guest in his wife's house and his real home is his sister's house.

(*d*) **Father-daughter**. Considered as the most ephemeral type of all, this preference for matrilocality stresses the economic relationship between the young man and his father-in-law.

(*e*) **Brother-sister**. Not very common, this system of residence norms is, however, typical among the Ashanti, in Ghana. Traditional preference goes to the household group composed of descendants from the same ancestor, whereas husband and wife live separately in their respective group. What is stressed here is the genealogical bond, which prevails over new ties in favour of brother and sister.

3.   *The size of the household*

Structure and residence are both qualitative identifiers. The size of the household is its prime quantitative characteristic, indicated by the number of individuals it contains. Numbers, however, can conceal qualitative diversity, assuming tacitly a homogeneity that only the de jure census creates. In most countries, censuses do not reflect correct marital status or non-marital cohabitation. Even if it can be reasonably assumed that census concepts of the household are generally comparable from one time and place to another, this mostly results from statistical standards all over the world. However, the concept may not fit the same reality everywhere, and may stand for the more versatile notion of family.

For convenience, however, current tables and past studies reporting household size and composition have mostly used simple ratios:

- Average household size: **P/H**

  P = total population, H = number of households, both undifferentiated

This information provides a rough idea of the average size, showing that throughout the developing countries differences among households are small and barely depart from the average of 5 persons per unit (Bongaarts, 2001). Household composition is indicative of the structure of the household in a given region, according to the breakdown by types of households.

The convention of assigning headship to the male in a husband-wife household corresponds less and less to reality in both developed and developing countries, where a process of modernization is taking place. A census, however, needs an individual reference, whether it is the "head of the household" with a more flexible definition or simply the "respondent".

Family headship is no longer a problem of gender. That paternalism, especially in the developed countries, belongs to the past does not mean that responsibilities automatically devolve to the woman. More and more, a new distribution of domestic obligations between the couple and a process of joint decision-making involving all members of the household occur. For instance, the decision to move may be taken after a discussion including the children and is concretized by the parents who work out its practical aspects. This is the reason why "headship" has become a term of reference rather than information on the composition of the family.

Currently, the crude headship rate is the inverse of the average household size:

- Crude headship rate: **H/P**

To investigate the composition of the average household, the following indicators are computed:

- Adult headship rate: **H/A**, where A = adult population

- The reciprocal of the adult headship rate is the number of adults per household: **A/H**

By using more detailed census data when available, it is possible to provide more useful indicators to identify family:

- Marital units per household, where "marital units" are the sum of married couples and widowed and divorced persons

- Households per married male: **H/M$_m$**

These indicators can be easily computed from readily available data.

As an illustration, by using these simple indicators, through the decomposition of the crude headship rate (H/P), it is possible to detect components of variation in average household size (Burch, 1987).

Let   H   =   number of households

A   =   number of adults (over age 15)

M   =   number of currently married persons

A$_m$ =   number of adult males

P   =   total population

Consequently, the headship rate is expressed through the measure of the prevalence of headship among married persons, the prevalence of marriage, the sex composition of the adult population and the age composition of the total population. However, not all household heads are married or males.

Then:

$$\mathbf{H/P} \quad = \quad (H/M) \, (M/A_m) \, (A_m/A) \, (A/P)$$

or

$$\mathbf{H/P} \quad = \quad (H/M_m) \, (M_m/A_m) \, (A_m/A) \, (A/P)$$

where M_m stands for the number of currently married males.

Each of these ratios is likely to be used as an indicator, bearing in mind the assumptions (Burch, 1987) on which they are necessarily based and that result from census limitations. This does not provide any information about broader, non-residential family or kinship structures. Similarly, the concept of household is not comparable from one time and place to another. In addition, the convention of assigning headship to the male in husband-wife households has already been pointed out.

Considering the structure of the household, household size should be computed according to the selected typology and the corresponding availability of data. The number of dyads, such as a single-mother unit with one child, but also with two, three or more children, in relation to household size by region could be calculated as data permit and presented in a detailed review of the households in their complexity. More generally, average size of household components such as the number of children and of adults, the number of spouses, the number of adult sons/daughters, and the number of related and unrelated persons should be calculated, whether by country or by region.

The size of the household components introduces what could be called associated indicators. These are variables highly correlated with size, meaning that their fluctuation has a definite correlation to the size of the household. However, this does not preclude an inverse relationship, so that these variables would be considered as interacting.

4. *Associated indicators*

Bongaarts (2001) proposed six proximate demographic determinants of the size of nuclear households: nuptiality, fertility, adoption, mortality, migration and divorce. As with any indicator, these should always be cautiously interpreted in the light of their approximation and the context they are meant to characterize.

(a) *Fertility*

Fertility level is regarded as highly correlated with the number of children in the household. For the purpose of designing indicators, it is assumed that the number of children not living in their mother's household is negligible and that infant mortality rates should give a sufficient indication of the effective fertility, since the number of children includes only survivors. Current fertility should be considered accurate enough. The **total fertility rate** (TFR) should therefore be an acceptable associated family indicator. In addition, Bongaarts showed that the number of children in the household was also adversely affected by the number of adults per household: the lower the propensity of adults to live together in the household, the higher the number of children.

(b) *Mortality*

Indicative of the current conditions concerning fertility is the **infant mortality rate** (or the child mortality rate, which is under five years of age, by sex). Although it fails to compare the deaths that occurred to the real population at risk (part of the infants dying this year were born last year, while part of the infants born this year are exposed to the risk of dying next year), it remains a good conventional indicator, mostly over a five-year period. When using in addition **life expectancy at birth** (the most frequently used indicator of living conditions), one should not forget the determinant weight of infant mortality that it reflects.

(c) *Marriage and the singulate mean age at marriage of women*

Since marriage or cohabitation usually represents a transfer of one adult to a new or different household, it is expected to induce a reorganization of the family. There is a highly significant correlation between the **singulate mean age at marriage of women** (SMAM) and the average number of adult daughters per household (Bongaarts, 2001). Contrasting this with males, who tend to leave the family home earlier, the women leave home at about the time they marry.

(d) *Age at first birth*

Information about the paths of change leading to the current characteristics of the family is usually difficult to obtain in any other way than through surveys. This is the case for the **mean age of mothers at first birth, by final parity**. This means in practice that women aged 50 and over are the reference persons. This cohort approach depends more on analysis than on the image an indicator might provide. It should be pointed out that the concept of cohorts is an external construct and is not based on a sense of participation. However, to the extent that data exist, the indicator would provide a historical account of the concentration process around the one- or two-child family norm.

(e) *Disruption and dissolution of the family*

Family is likely to disappear or to assume a new shape through divorce, separation or the death of one or both spouses. In developed countries, and where marriage is still the common union, data exist about the **yearly number of divorces**, although the information remains indicative of further disruption in conjugal status. This is, therefore, a partial indicator, which reveals the fragility of the institution, increasingly bypassed by a process of cohabitation that may or may not lead to marriage or residential permanency.

The **current number of widows** attests to past dissolutions of a family. Additional information by sex and age plus the duration of the union is useful but not likely to provide simple indicators on households. In a more general way, the **proportion of heads that do not live with a spouse** (Bongaarts, 2001) can be used as an indirect indicator of marital disruption.

(f) *Migration*

Migration is a disruptive factor whose importance has been growing, not only because of the population volumes it involves, but also because of changing and diversifying patterns concerning the invoked or real reasons for moving from one location to another. Since these movements are not entirely registered, as exemplified by clandestine migration, which has increased significantly in the recent past, or by the numbers of displaced persons living in temporary conditions that may actually last for decades, it is extremely difficult to assess the effects on the household. It has been shown that internal migration and new labour mobility have caused the family to converge to a nuclear model. Nevertheless, in developing areas, rural-urban migration has affected the size of the household in relation with compelling lineage bonds, which have obligated the migrant to take care of his/her relatives in his/her new environment as soon as the economic situation has shown an improvement.

As proximate data, the percentage of the population in rural and urban areas and in the main cities, shown by changes in the distribution of these populations, may offer evidence of migratory flows (magnitude and pattern in time). The proportion of births by age to mothers of reproductive age who were born outside a given territory may provide an indication of the magnitude of past migrations and their effects on household composition.

(g) *Age distribution of the population by gender*

The relative volume of different age groups in the total population indicates various activities that are determined by age, such as the economic dependence of children and persons over 65 years of age.

C. FAMILY DYNAMICS

Over the last few decades, men have been the conservative element of the institutional family, releasing bit by bit their hold on a "shrinking territory". It seems therefore more justified to approach family change from the woman's perspective, using the lens of the history of emancipation. Women have had a much greater influence on the changes that family structures have undergone. Increasing participation in the workforce, easier access to more reliable contraceptives and feminist ideas have reshaped the concept of family to a great degree. The perennial view of the nuclear family as a unit consisting of a male breadwinner, a wife who stays at home full-time and their children has been comprehensively altered by social change that is documented in recent census information.

Today's woman is a new kind of partner, radically altering an image shaped throughout history by the dominant role of men in society. New relations have evolved between the sexes that have affected the family and the household as a centre of shared income. The question that has arisen out of this sudden but quiet revolution is: What are the significant variables of this change?

In addition to the transformation of gender relationships that has led couples to consider any marital contract as an instrument of transitory stability, as expressed by a growing number of cohabiting couples (although Scandinavia has recently been showing a clear trend towards the rehabilitation of marriage) and a decline in fertility, other factors have played a major role in changing the intrinsic nature of the links between members of the family. Even when the shape of the family conforms to its nuclear pattern, it has nevertheless exhibited a growing independence at the individual level. This should be seen as exclusively the accomplishment of the woman, whose emancipation has extended to various realms, from politics and equal rights to a striving for economic equality that includes access to education, employment and income.

28

Higher education has been provided to an increasing number of women, preparing them for a remunerated career. While men have usually been seen as the providers of the family and often remained cast as such, women feel free to dedicate themselves to a career and find their identity outside of the home. These are the trends that have helped to alter the image of the family. Homogeneity, however, is never the rule in societies. A gender-based typology proposed by Keuzenkamp in 1994 (see Frinking, 1995) includes the following variables for measuring the attitudes of women towards employment and family:

- **Women mostly turned towards employment**. These women work full-time, are often divorced or single and have fewer children (when they have more than three children it is exceptional).

- **Women mostly turned towards family**. Most of the time, these women have no professional activities or part-time work. The proportion of married (or remarried) women is higher, and they have higher fertility.

- **Women with a double orientation**. These women usually work full-time, but have a family life.

External conditions are likely to modify these categories. For example, the situation of the labour market may be determined by changing the rules to benefit working men. Family policy may determine alterations in the behaviour of women, who may for a while postpone their career ambitions while benefiting from childcare allowances. These factors, therefore, should constitute additional associated indicators.

In addition to the TFR and the SMAM, the following data could describe a context, favourable or unfavourable, concerning the activity of women in conjunction with family change:

- Ratio of girls compared to boys enrolled in secondary and post-secondary education (including professional teaching);

- Proportion of women in paid non-farm jobs;

- Unemployment rate by sex (and age groups);

- Measures taken by the Government that are likely to affect the labour market for women and the family (special allowances, number of day-care centres etc.);

- Average wages by sex, age groups and levels of education, by occupation.

CONCLUSION

The attempt to conceptualize indicators offering a quantitative analysis of the family seems to have led to unexpected conclusions. The definition of the family, instead of focusing on indicators specifying the nature of the family and defining accurately its role and possibilities, has become more imprecise. Only some of the avenues for analysis seem potentially useful. The intended structure of indicators, which is not an instrument for detecting relationships, can offer only an approximation to reality.

The lack of data about the family appears to be a serious obstacle. However, the main difficulty lies in the need to define clearly what a family is. The concept, which is not universal, displays many variations. Arriving at a precise definition has proved difficult, whether in developed or developing countries. As a result, a simple quantitative approach does not seem to offer a solution to the problem.

In the end, family is a social construct, a form of union whose legitimacy rests on legal acknowledgement and which represents an effort to institutionalize a series of facts, some biological (conception, regulated sexuality) and others affective (affinities in the couple, adoption).

Throughout the text, an attempt has been made to characterize the concept of family by a set of indicators, most of them already in use. The difficulty of proving the existence of the family, as distinct from the household (which may seem paradoxical inasmuch as the household was described for convenience and for approximation as a statistical unit in place of the family), is evident. Ultimately, the only statistical reality is the household, while the family is an institution defined by social and political choice. In this case, indicators can only express choices that the law or custom have legitimated through the institutions of society. From this perspective, the family can be only what the society deems best in order to maintain its structure, and as such is the result of customs and policies.

REFERENCES

Bohannan, Paul (1968). An alternate residence classification. In *Marriage, Family and Residence*, P. Bohannan and J. Middleton, eds. New York: The Natural History Press.

Bongaarts, J., T. K. Burch and K. Wachter, eds. (1987). *Family Demography: Methods and Their Applications.* Oxford, United Kingdom: Clarendon Press.

Bongaarts, John (2001). Household size and composition in the developing world. Policy Research Division Working Paper No. 144. New York: The Population Council.

Burch, Thomas (1987). Measures of household composition and headship based on aggregate routine census data. In *Family Demography: Methods and Their Applications,* J. Bongaarts, T. K. Burch and K. Wachter, eds. Oxford, United Kingdom: Clarendon Press.

Fabri, Marcel (1982). Interdisciplinaritatea, concept si aplicatie. *Vitorule Social*, Revista de Sociologie si stiinue politice. Bucureşti, Editura Academiei Republicii Socialiste Romania.

_____ (1990). *La politique de population tunisienne en perspective.* Tunis: Ministère du plan et du développement régional de Tunisie, Institut de recherches et d'études sur la population (IREP).

Frinking, Gérard (1995). Emancipation et famille. In *La sociologie des populations*, Hubert Gérard and Victor Piché, eds. Montréal: Les Presses de l'Université de Montréal.

Galtung, J., D. Poleszinski and A. Wirak (1978). Indicators for development. Paper for United Nations University, Goals, Processes and Indicators of Development (GPID) project (1978-1982).

Goodenough, Ward H. (1968). Residence rules. In *Marriage, Family and Residence*, P. Bohannan and J. Middleton, eds. New York: The Natural History Press.

Goody, Jack (1990). Future of the family in rural Africa. In *Rural Development and Population: Institutions and Policy*, Geoffrey McNicoll and Mead Cain, eds. Oxford and New York: Oxford University Press.

Gruenais, M.-E. (1981). *Famille et démographie de la famille en Afrique.* Paris: Institut français de recherche scientifique pour le développement en coopération (ORSTOM).

International Union for the Scientific Study of Population (IUSSP) (1982). *Multilingual Demographic Dictionary*, 2nd edition. Liège, Belgium: Ordina Editions.

Leridon, Henri, and C. Villeneuve-Gokalp (1994). Family continuities and discontinuities: family life histories of couples and children. Travaux et Documents, Cahier No. 134. Paris: Institut National d'Etudes Démographiques (INED).

Loriaux, Michel (1982). Occupation, social status, class: a winning bet for sociology? Concerning the good and bad use of terminologies and occupational categories, prestige, hierarchies, status indexes, and measures of class. In *Populations et structures sociales: Chaire Quetelet* 1981. Louvain-la-Neuve, Belgium: Université Catholique de Louvain.

Roussel, A. (1980). Propositions pour une recherche transversale de démographie familiale. In *Une nouvelle façon d'aborder la coopération dans la recherche démographique*, vol. 2. Paris: Committee for International Cooperation in National Research in Demography (CICRED).

Ryder, Norman B. (1977). Models of family demography. *Population Bulletin of the United Nations*, No. 9.

Tilly, Charles (1964). *The Vendée*. Cambridge, Massachusetts: Harvard University Press.

United Nations (1980). *Principles and Recommendations for Population and Housing Censuses*, Statistical Papers Series M, No. 67. Sales No. E.80.XVII.8.

_____ (1995). *The World's Women: Trends and Statistics*. Social Statistics and Indicators Series K, No. 12. Sales No. E.95.XVII.2.

_____ (2000). *The World's Women: Trends and Statistics*. Social Statistics and Indicators Series K, No. 16. Sales No. E.00.XVII.14.

Wolf, Eric R. (1966). *Peasants*. Englewood Cliffs, New Jersey: Prentice-Hall.

_____ (1969). *Peasant Wars of the Twentieth Century*. New York: Harper and Row.

ANNEX I

Proposals for a typology of family[a]

0. Households without any family, including:

    0.1 Households represented by one person
    8 sub-types (2 sexes x 4 marital statuses)
    0.2 Households represented by one ascendant and one child aged 25 or over
    0.3 Other households without any family

1. Households formed by one family only:

    1.1 Households without any isolated person:[b]
        1.1.1 Couples without children
            1.1.1.1 Married couples
            1.1.1.2 Non-married couples
        1.1.2 Couples with non-married children under 25 years of age
            1.1.2.1 Married couples
            1.1.2.2 Non-married couples
        1.1.3 One adult without spouse with at least one non-married child under 25 years old (8 sub-types as for 0.1)

    1.2 Households with at least one isolated person:[b]
        1.2.1 Couples without children with one ascendant
        1.2.1 Couples with at least one child aged 25 or over
        1.2.3 Couples with another constellation of isolated persons
        1.2.4 Households with children aged under 25 years plus one ascendant
        1.2.5 Households with children aged under 25 years plus at least one child aged over 25 years
        1.2.6 Households with children aged under 25 years plus another constellation of isolated persons
        1.2.7 An adult without spouse with children aged under 25 years plus one ascendant
        1.2.8 An adult without spouse with children aged under 25 years plus a child of 25 years or over
        1.2.9 An adult without spouse with children aged under 25 years plus another constellation

---

[a]A. Roussel, "Propositions pour une recherche transversale de démographie familiale", in *Une nouvelle façon d'aborder la coopération dans la recherche démographique*, vol. 2 (Paris, Committee for International Cooperation in National Research in Demography [CICRED], 1980), p. 52.
[b]Other than father, mother or children under 25.

2. Households formed by two families:

    2.1 The receiving family is that of the ascendants
        2.1.1   Without any isolated persons
        2.1.2   With isolated persons

    2.2 The receiving family is that of the descendants
        2.2.1   Without any isolated persons
        2.2.2   With isolated persons
        2.2.3   Other households composed of two families

3. Households formed by more than two families

ANNEX II

Provisional programme for tabulation
for each type of household[a]

TYPE OF HOUSEHOLD[b]

01	Sex/marital status/age/economically active and non-economically active
02	Sex of the ascendant/age of the ascendant/number of children
03	Size of the household
04	id
05	id
1111	Age of the man/age of the woman
	Age of the man/socio-professional category of the man/socio-professional category of the woman
	Age of the woman/socio-professional category of the woman
1112	The same three tables as for 1111
1121	The same three tables as for 1111 and age of the woman/economically active—non-economically active/number of children
1122	The same four tables as for 1121
113	Sex/marital status/age/economically active—economically inactive
121	Age of the ascendant/age of the man in the couple
122	Age of the father/number of children aged 25 years and over
123	Age of the man in the couple/size of the household
124	Age of the man in the couple/age of the woman in the couple
125	Age of the man in the couple/number of children aged 25 years and over
126	Age of the man in the couple/size of the household
127	Sex/marital status/age of the adult
128	id
129	id
211	Age of the head of the ascendant family/number of children of the descendant family/size of the household
212	id
221	id
222	id
23	Size of the household

[a]National Institute of Demographic Studies (INED) and National Institute of Statistics and Economic Studies (INSEE), Paris, October 1979.
[b]A. Roussel, "Propositions pour une recherche transversale de démographie familiale", in *Une nouvelle façon d'aborder la coopération dans la recherche démographique*, vol. 2 (Paris, Committee for International Cooperation in National Research in Demography [CICRED], 1980), p. 53.

ANNEX III

Households classified by type[a]

Households can be classified according to the following types:

1. One-person household;

2. Nuclear household, defined as a household consisting entirely of a single family nucleus;

3. Extended household, defined as a household consisting of either:
    (*a*) A single family nucleus and other persons related to the nucleus;
    (*b*) Two or more family nuclei related to each other, without any other persons;
    (*c*) Two or more family nuclei related to each other plus other persons related to at least one of the nuclei; or
    (*d*) Two or more persons related to each other but none of whom comprises a family nucleus;

4. Composite household, defined as a household consisting of either:
    (*a*) A single family nucleus plus other persons, some of whom are related to the nucleus and some of whom are not;
    (*b*) A single family nucleus plus other persons, none of whom is related to the nucleus;
    (*c*) Two or more family nuclei related to each other plus other persons, some of whom are related to at least one of the nuclei and some of whom are not related to any of the nuclei;
    (*d*) Two or more family nuclei related to each other plus other persons, none of whom is related to any of the nuclei;
    (*e*) Two or more family nuclei not related to each other, with or without any other persons;
    (*f*) Two or more persons related to each other but none of whom comprises a family nucleus, plus other unrelated persons; or
    (*g*) Non-related persons only.

---

[a]*Principles and Recommendations for Housing Censuses* (United Nations publication, Sales No. E.80.XVII.8), para. 2.84.

كيفية الحصول على منشورات الأمم المتحدة

يمكن الحصول على منشورات الأمم المتحدة من المكتبات ودور التوزيع في جميع أنحاء العالم . استعلم عنها من المكتبة
التي تتعامل معها أو اكتب إلى : الأمم المتحدة ، قسم البيع في نيويورك أو في جنيف .

如何购取联合国出版物

联合国出版物在全世界各地的书店和经售处均有发售。请向书店询问或写信到纽约或日内瓦的
联合国销售组。

HOW TO OBTAIN UNITED NATIONS PUBLICATIONS

United Nations publications may be obtained from bookstores and distributors throughout the
world. Consult your bookstore or write to: United Nations, Sales Section, New York or Geneva.

COMMENT SE PROCURER LES PUBLICATIONS DES NATIONS UNIES

Les publications des Nations Unies sont en vente dans les librairies et les agences dépositaires
du monde entier. Informez-vous auprès de votre libraire ou adressez-vous à : Nations Unies,
Section des ventes, New York ou Genève.

КАК ПОЛУЧИТЬ ИЗДАНИЯ ОРГАНИЗАЦИИ ОБЪЕДИНЕННЫХ НАЦИЙ

Издания Организации Объединенных Наций можно купить в книжных магазинах
и агентствах во всех районах мира. Наводите справки об изданиях в вашем книжном
магазине или пишите по адресу: Организация Объединенных Наций, Секция по
продаже изданий, Нью-Йорк или Женева.

COMO CONSEGUIR PUBLICACIONES DE LAS NACIONES UNIDAS

Las publicaciones de las Naciones Unidas están en venta en librerías y casas distribuidoras en
todas partes del mundo. Consulte a su librero o diríjase a: Naciones Unidas, Sección de Ventas,
Nueva York o Ginebra.

Litho in United Nations, New York
02-69862—April 2003—2,025
ISBN 92-1-130225-0

United Nations publication
Sales No. E.03.IV.4
ST/ESA/279